THE BONE-JOINER

by Sandi Leibowitz

Sycorax Press
New York

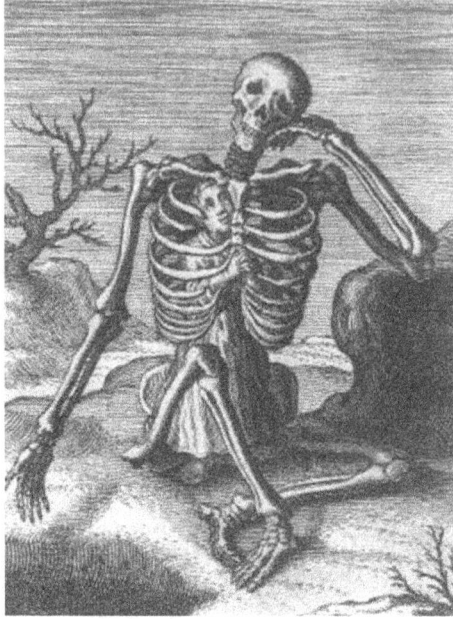

Published by Sycorax Press
New York

ISBN 10-0999883909
ISBN-13-978-0-9998839-0-7

Cover art: *The Penitent Magdalene* – Georges de La Tour –
Metropolitan Museum of Art
Copyright page art: *Kind in skelet van de Dood gekropen* – Boetius Adamsz—
Rijksmuseum

THE BONE-JOINER

Contents

I.   Witch-Love

The Bone-Joiner   7
Ah, Joringel!   10
The Gifts   12
Dr. Chadpur Goes Fishing in the Animasphere   14
On Failure's Wings   16
Birdspell   19
Ephemera   24
Sun-Taste   26
Sycorax Awaits the Birth of Caliban   27
Witch-Love   30

II.   Lady Mary Speaks of Dreams

Sleeping Gypsy   35
Lady Mary Speaks of Dreams   37
Im Wald   39
A Ballad of the Northlands   42
The Last Mouse   44
The Daughter of Lir   45
One-Winged   47
The Island of Crows   49

III. Awakened

Entreaty   53
Ariel's Release   54
Seeds of Love   56
Noticed   57
Labyrinth of Sand   59
Lizzie Siddal's Blessing   62
To a Gentleman Who is Visited   64

Lapis Lazuli   66
Awakened   67

IV. Invasion

The Art   71
The Mummy Bared   73
Kosode-No-Te   75
The Cat Accursed   77
Old Bone   78
Rusalka   80
Max in Wolf-Suit   81
Invasion   84

V. Attic Dust

The Emperor's Clockwork Song-Bird   87
Making Home   89
Attuned   91
Braiding   93
Straw Man   96
Psyche's Lamp   98
Penemue   99
The Five Books   101
The Man Who Loved a Poem   103
Poppet Piracy   105
Chopin's Heart   106
Deliberate Imperfection   108
Attic Dust   110

Acknowledgements   113

About the Author   115

I. Witch-Love

The Bone-Joiner

The music stirs
as this rib slips into its slot of spine,
a perfect fit.
Eyes closed, I work the puzzle
of the skeleton; with opened eyes
I'd guess and flub, each marring
jar the humming out of tune.

They sing, the bones, when they find
their place,
duet at first when part meets part
and then the swell of chorus
as my work grows whole.

Watching, she waits, the widow,
wide-eyed now and hollow as straw,
without the strength she used to row the skiff
that brought him to me.

The bargain struck,
she'd cradled the corpse on her lap like a babe,
gave herself up to weeping
till I pried her fingers loose
and took him to the fire.

She would not heed me then,
pretended maybe it was only stew
a-bubbling in the pot.
Ah no, the seekers cringe from dissolution,
no matter how well they know
my art requires destroying
before creation can begin.

But now, as I join, she observes,
listening to the clack of bone on bone,
like the tune of knitting needles.

Does she recognize this empty cage
that held the heart she prized?
Do these large fingers, unringed and unfleshed,
recall the ones that laced with hers?

Soon I'll pour the brew
to clothe these bones again.
He'll groan,
eyes flutter open,
lips smile to find her there.

Between the seeker and beloved
the air will hum,
a new harmony.

Is that what love is, then,
deep in the bone,
a music that fits one to another?

I know of bones
but I don't know this.

When I breathe my last,
no one will care to bring me back,
fit me together rib by rib,
and I cannot fathom loving anyone
enough to wake them.
Perhaps all joiners own this flaw,
so we may go brisk about our business
with a surgeon's ease.

But always the seekers come to me,
children sometimes, mothers often,
lovers most of all, they come as she has come,
bones aching with soul's need.

In an hour or two, he'll gasp and gulp.
She'll clasp him round the waist

and rush him to the skiff,
hurrying from my dreadful isle
towards home.

I'll never know the story after,
what dreams may grasp him
in the dead of night,
whether someday she'll grow to loathe
that cold flesh in her arms,
or if—the tale I tell myself
through all the silent nights—
they'll learn an even truer love and kinder.

Long before sun sets, the sea
will wash their footsteps
from my shore

and I will only hear the hum of surf,
wind rattling the dead trees' bones.

Ah, Joringel!

My pearl, my gem,
My red flower!

The years ticked by while I
modeled marble out of men,
composed birds from
the raw stuff of girls.
One well-wrought chant
and blue veins hardened into white,
over-loud hearts
muffled within travertine.
I molted jut of chin
and droop of breast
into exactitude of
thrush and wren.

Who can explain the itch
of the collector?
Crowding my garden with statues
and my tower with cages,
for you I waited,
you of the poppy-soft skin,
you of the apple-sweet mouth.

Ah, Joringel,
My one in seven thousand!

My tower's loud with song;
the larks trill for freedom,
the swallows warble dirges
that would make black horses waltz.
But it's Jorinda,
your nightingale, your love,
who tunes the day to dawn.
I cannot sing so sweet.
My songs hoot and croak.

Ah, Joringel,
My pearl, my gem,
My flower red as blood!

The tower-clock keeps
a placid face
while Time screams on.
Even so am I
the stillness at the center
of sorcery's undoing,
the wings shuddering back
into shoulders,
the shattering stone.
I give you my best gift,
a dream that bursts the bars.

How the crimson petals
Enfold the pearl!

I set you free
and I become
the cat, the owl, the witch,
the dark thing in the night,
the tattered hag that mutters to her demons,
O Zachiel! the moon!,
the forest's black wings.

The Gifts

For Sara Cleto and Brittany Warman

The sisters parted
once the gifts were given.
No need now to thread their lives
through a single needle;
each had her own path to stitch.

The younger one loved spring best
so her work spilled grape hyacinths
into the winter meadows,
made blue waves swim
onto the white cloth of frozen rivers.
From her needle bloomed larkspur,
columbine and the tendrils of sweet pea
curled like napping mouselings.

She embroidered rainfall,
never harsh and pelting but
silver droplets,
and beaded moonstone dew
onto the morning grass.

The elder preferred the forest
by night.
She stitched moss
out of shadow-threads
and gifted golden eyes
to the hunting owls.
Her needle pricked new stars
in the fabric of the sky
to light the trails of wolves.

Will-o-the-wisps and witches
blessed her for her subtle shadings,
pewters and slates

silvering the sables.
She threaded fox-bark and bat-cry
to make hammocks
for the luna moths,
embroidered dreams
for the elms and oaks,
who sighed in their sleeping,
rustling leaves in canine frenzy
as they leaped and loped
free of their roots.

The sisters never met again,
but the elder smiled to find
crocuses shining like a ring of lamps
around her midnight thicket,
the younger rejoiced at the canopies
of Spanish moss sewn amongst
her plum blossoms.

Dr. Chadpur Goes Fishing in the Animasphere

Black's what I see first
when I peer into the depths,
before I catch the silver swimmers,
underglints of cyan or amber
—the shadings of each separate soul—
my ethereal jellyfish.

Demure Anemone, tendrils of pink
blushing to crimson, forces
a foreign tenderness into my heart.
Tempest, pulsating galaxy,
encourages in me a dreadful urge to shout.

I curse this tendency to name them.
I must ignore the stirring of my own spirit
as Golden Sparrow or Purple Koi flits past.
They are not pets.
As man of science I recognize
my mind's habit of personification.
I must refrain.

Think of mermaids.
They were just reflections, after all,
of the human desire to meet unearthly beauty,
men's desire to possess in woman-form
the subtle shapeliness of the sea.

I cast my line,
trail my metaphysical hook
in circles, skips and starts,
like any fisherman his bait.
We don't know yet why
some souls choose
to answer this invitation.

Those re-vivified remember nothing
of the life-between.

Do they guess my purpose?
Hunger for a second life,
or selflessly decide to serve?
Do they sense *me?*

I only know that some souls leap
to my line, eager—
it's these I'll tug
toward second corporeality—
while others flee.

Nagini, emerald temptress,
seems to sniff my line
before she darts away.
I war with myself,
yearning to catch her,
yet also wishing her to remain free,
roaming the Animasphere at will.

When I began, it was Science
I served, and humanity,
granting resurrection of a kind
to the comatose.

But I must admit that now
it is the act of fishing I love most,
observing the dance of souls
within the Great Bowl,
waiting for the tug of the line.

On Failure's Wings

"Create something beautiful,"
you say.
Never mind how hard it is to break
a form's desire to remain itself, convince it
to betray its purpose,
knead almost-nothing into a live being.

I stifle the—not excuses!
Explanations!
You've never studied
the tripartite Laws of Hermegistus,
the Transformation Modalities,
cannot guess how difficult...

I kneel,
scoop a handful of dirt, spit into my palm,
mold the pellet of mud,
my will forming and enlarging the ball,
shaping,
heating.
I sweat as I kindle from the inert mass
a spark.

It steps forth from my hands,
landing at your feet.

Poor little flop-headed thing,
ugly as an unfledged chick,
no peacock, let alone a phoenix.
Even a year's maturation
would never lend it grace.
Disappointment slithers across your face.

The Making shudders as if
encountering a cobra.
It swivels its ungainly neck,

raises mournful, hopeful eyes
to me.

You asked me to make you something beautiful.
I want to ask,
Are we not enough,
this *we* we've built?
Or am I wrong about this, too,
believe myself co-architect
of a gold and many-towered palace,
while I bide alone in an englamoured hut?

Within my breast,
my love sings whole and hale,
more rapturous beautiful
than any magicked Making.
See how it spreads wide its red and golden wings,
and, talons stretched, ruby eyes seeking only you,
flies towards your heart
with a raptor's unerring navigation?
Can you not feel its flames
ignite the air
that separates your body from mine?

The unfeathered stubs of my Making
shudder and jerk as it flops
its exhausting inches towards me.

Creator,
it almost speaks,
accept me as I am.

It flinches even as its eyes plead,
seeing,
—before I've done it,
before you speed through the arbor
like a galleon abandoning a plague port —

my hands snap its neck.

I don't take time to counsel
this child of my inconsequential powers,
instruct it like a good father should:
Every phoenix, even those ill-formed,
must abide destruction.

Even so each lover
daily must rebuild his dream
out of the ashes of his heart.

Birdspell

I.

The gift of a sparrow
ensures three hours
of happiness,
beyond which
you are on your own,
the spell collapses like
a candle snuffed

I've sent you seven cages
filled with sparrows
Set them free
and let your darkness lighten

Maybe then your heart
will have learned
to sing on its own

II.

The nightingale is a mourner,
her own elegist.
It is no easy task
to kill a nightingale—
not hard to capture,
but the act itself,
willing oneself to jab the spear
into the innocent breast,
requires courage

Split open the bird
while she still breathes
If she is singing,
even better

Her blood on your hands
helps—one *should* rue murder
Red hands mean wild hearts
capable of anything

Skewer the beating heart,
roast it in a bonfire
and eat

Your songs will now be bloodier,
meatier,
their pain more believable
Your lover may turn to you because of them

This was my hope

I killed and I ate

III.

Paper birds are promises
White cranes promise health,
cardinals passion,
blue jays hope

I folded one hundred
blue and red paper birds,
spread on them the blood
of the dead nightingale

and watched them take the air

The wind devoured the jays,
crashed the cardinals
to the pavement

Why, my sparrow,

do you prefer your cage
to my garden?
Why isn't my love enough
to set you free?

IV.

Black swans are what monsters
dream themselves to be,
improbably beautiful,
dramatic as sin or tragedy

Shall I not float
like a blossom
on a lake?
bewails the ogre

Shall I not quench my fire
in shadow lustrous as soul-soot?
laments the djinn

Why may I not entwine
my neck with the neck
of my beloved?
the griffin grieves

I dream we are black swans,
my sparrow-love

V.

The fan of the peacock's tail
is a screen
hiding all his secrets,
every murder or infidelity

Each one's a Bluebeard

skilled in legerdemain
willing you to watch the fan
and miss the trick

Are you a peacock, my sparrow?

VI.

Owls are the purest of birds
When I was an owl
they called me Death
the purest thing of all

Sparrow-heart, I changed you
to a dove
not for their chastity,
which is a lie,
but because the dove
is irresistible to the owl
as buddleia to butterfly

I wanted to taste
your surrender
while you were swathed
in spotless plumage,
your last breath veiled
in bridal white

VII.

They rise as a cloud of green
from dream-rivers,
nameless,
a flock of birds-that-would-be,
birds-that-never-were.
You see them and your heart
flutters its own wings in time.

They are paradise writ
in bone and feather and song.
This was the dream you told me,
sparrow-heart,
the birds were your own doing

I fold green-paper flocks
and whistle my improper tunes
to conjure your dream-birds awake,
hoping they will take me
to your paradise
but all my promptings come to naught

I have lost my wings
I have lost my voice
and you, if you sing somewhere,
will not sing of me

Ephemera

The scent of her green,
fern fronds trembling in tree shade,
apple leaves cupping the pink cheeks of blossoms,
nocturnal pines.

I open the slender flask and breathe her in;
absinthe-hued fumes rise to take her shape.

I carry you, my dead dears,
in my pocket,
the clink of glass on glass
—always the titillating risk of breakage—
a fragile calliope chorusing
your presence.

I unstopper your flask:
you come to me at your loveliest best,
without demands or chatter,
no pride or pouting,
no woeful slide to wrinkled age or
padded silhouette.

A quick blade to the throat,
insistent as the act of love,
and your sweet essence
poured into my bottle,
mine forever,
freed of all the fripperies
of flesh.

Tomorrow night, let me inhale
the heady bergamot of the Romani dancer,
scarlet musk of my late Spaniard wife,
chaste lavender of that coy English maid,
or indulge in violet fancies of an amour

two decades old but ever fresh,
attar of Rose.

Sun-Taste

Let me kiss the last amber drops
that bead your lip.
My tongue shares the sweetness,
honey-thick but electric,
more alive than whiskey's
hot ride down the throat.

I have fed you one taste of
light's last golden shout
before night shutters the sky.

Now the bright orb of your heart
blazes like spring's shift into summer,
your blood sings the birds'
cries at afternoon's surrender,
that moment when becoming meets gone,
the last breath of the pupa as
the first wingtip unfolds.

Sycorax Awaits the Birth of Caliban

spine grows soft like island pine;
ankles swell;
breath comes short;
blue vines of veins
trellis my trunks.

hagseed thumps,
kicks its heels
as once I did mine in Algiers,
widow-wild before this sowing
unmagicked me.

I still could coax the comelies,
glamoured to unsee
raisined dugs and loose teeth slanty.
Sycorax has herbs turns
all us girls buxom
but sometimes didn't even need 'em;
these mans can see past any fault if given
the little magick of groin honey.

not market buzz I miss,
but brasslamps' dazzle,
cardamom whiff,
the oud and tambourine.
here be better,
not hateful human yaps,
no manstench, but
blue coves for sinking
sweating hagflesh into.
Here polite palms bow me lady.
Sycorax be island's queen,
no soldiers to drum her
out of taverns' doors
or club her bones.

o brave new world,
that has no people in it!
only night-padding wolves,
owls moony-eyed,
prickly 'pines of savory meat,
crabs beetle-bummed,
and flitty spirits I call up
to hum and sing
when memories grow gnawsome.
here winds be tame
and summer-sweet
and there be plenty
fish to eat.

I lean against this
cedar with relief,
watch the waves,
wait to whelp and
wonder what fruit will fall
from this me tree.
will it have bright eyes brown
like smooth hipped sailors
or hot red wings,
sweet piercing fangs?

I, dam of you unborn,
do promise now to
teach you never
no manthings!
but how to hunt like hawk,
enjoy devour.
words be honeypoison,
net you, harm you.
better know catchings
of cunning conies,
roots to heal hurts.

meanwhile, I rock you moon's eye

red from dreaming hag-hex,
I rock you river-growl
and ravensong.
but no more words.

Algiers far's no longer missed.
ocean mews
my hagseed safe in its nest.

Witch-Love

When the witch married the sea,
she slept on beds of kelp
and barked in otter-tongue.
She wove capes of tender weeds
and danced widdershins
in the foamy wakes of whales.
Pearls were as common as pennies;
if she wanted to feel rich
she counted all the ocean's greens,
her tongue a clapper in the bell
of the world, chiming their names.

When the witch married the stone,
she learned it is no sin to be hard.
If she craved softness,
she gloved herself in velvet lichens,
coaxed a sparrow to brush its wing
against her bulk.
She studied the fine art of time and tarry.
She tasted weather but ignored it,
suffering nothing from sleet and snow
except the subtle shiftings of the earth
beneath her form.
Erosion barely pained her till
one winter's contraction
cracked her.

When the witch married the wind,
she broke free of the field and fled
to woods and wilds, revisited the sea.
She toured the cities,
every tower and alley.
For kicks she became a thief of hats,
a gambler betting on the races
between tumbling newspaper rivals.
She was an artist then:

all through the winter nights
she practiced her singing;
in the summers she danced
dust-storms and tornadoes.

When the witch married the night,
she rose above day's fret and fever,
tuned herself to hear the planets'
subtle harmonies beyond the silence.
She sculpted faces in the moon.
She began to forget the world below,
which she had loved in many forms.
When star-fire called to her,
she came,
became pure flame,
a passion that never knew
surcease of burning.

II. Lady Mary Speaks of Dreams

Sleeping Gypsy

(After Henri Rousseau)

Was it the moon or your mandolin
that coaxed me from your dreams?
Did your long brown fingers,
remembering the strings,
pull me forth from the dream-threads,
strand by silver strand of mane?

Or was it the long-necked jug,
its belly full of sweet-water,
that called with a dusty throat,
'Wander from the moon-strands,
o beast of the dream-dunes,
beast of desert sighs,
and walk the world'?

You journeyed long, gypsy,
your bare feet burned,
before you earned your rest.
You stowed your dun blanket
beneath your weary head
and lay down,
staff still gripped at your side.

How soon, how soon,
the dreams flowed forth,
their rainbow dyeing your pillow,
your robes,
summoning a river
to flow beside you
and the dunes to rise up
as hills.

Soon I will leave you,
far traveler,

for my heart already leaps
to the unnamed hills
even as the gold orbs of my eyes
linger on your slumbering form,
my nostrils breathe in the cardamom
of your night-dark skin.

But first I will sing to you
of the moon,
the wind-blessed lands of blue trees
where silver cubs chase
the stars each night.

You will waken, my gypsy,
and know me,
even after I've gone.
Your soul will leap to my singing,
your mandolin will wake,
the desert will sigh
to the quiver of your strings.

Lady Mary Speaks of Dreams

In my dreams, Mr. Fox,
I rescue you.

Every night resurrects
not our aborted wedding
but afterwards,
white skin against white skin,
a sea of red fox-pelts
warm under us.

I grow bold, grow bold.
My hand reaches out
—in my dreams, Mr. Fox—
to caress a tail's length
to its white tip,
then moves to your chest.

That unreined beast,
your heart,
gallops under my finger tips,
in my dreams.

But by day, memory wakes.
Before my first yawn
she proffers garlands of
ringed fingers bound with
red silks and blonde.

In the gardens I discover
no peace, just ardent bees
amuck in jeweled melons' ruin,
wings enfeebled by sticky liquor,
immured in sweet flesh
become catacombs.

Such secret chambers haunt me:

your mind, locked against me,
my body's own forbidden place
that you will never enter.

My heart's blood runs cold.

Im Wald

"This is how I'll find you,"
you said.
You pointed to the broken twigs
fallen to the snow's belly,
trees' detritus.
I tried to believe they meant something.

One kiss—your warm mouth
burned my blue lips—
and you were gone.
I wanted to follow in your tread
like the page in the carol.

The night before,
our breath smoked upward
like escaping souls.

The wolves howled. White screams.
 "They mean to devour us with fear!"
I whimpered.

"Oh, no, *mädchen,* they're singing joy!
Joy in the night, the woods,
the blood that runs warm through their veins
though all the world is cold.
Would you blame a thing that sings?"

Your voice strung a filament of song
from tree to tree.
I swear it woke the icy stars
and made them wink encouragement.

You rubbed my frozen hands.
Through my gloves I felt
the holes worn through the wool of yours.
Poor boy, I thought, dressed in rags.

In the dawn you left.
Now I wander through the snow alone.
At night I pretend the stars
are Hansel's stones, leading home.

Such pretty lies.
My home is gone, my village
and my people.
All I have left is the mere hope of you,
the stranger in the woods
playing a game of hero.

At night I gather twigs and branches,
light them as you taught me,
sing your star-song to keep
the wolves and frost at bay.

The trees shimmer with ice
like Ashenputtel's lovely mother,
her grandmamma and aunts
attired in ballgowns and brilliants.
They float, they float,
to the hum of the wind
and someone's wild singing.

Mother Holle fluffs her feather quilt.
I would lie quiet underneath.
But, foolishly, I sing your song
believing you will come
before starvation or the soldiers do.

By day I walk.
I can barely place
one foot before the next.
So hungry.
I sit beneath this tree
a little while,
smell nutmeg rising from the pine bark.

I wake-dream of a gingerbread hut.
The witch's glowing oven seems
a pleasant means to death.
I will expire with a smile
like the little match girl,
dreaming of fire.

I look out at the black twigs on white snow.
How had I failed to notice until now
that they're laid out like staffs of music,
like the pages Papa played from
long ago?

On the sheet of snow,
the twig-notes rustle.
An alarm?
I hear an ocean sound—
waves of wings.
A great murder heads towards me,
humming your twig-tune,
their black forms look like notes
against the paper-white sky.

Steaming bread they carry
in their beaks
and from one crow's claws
your red mittens dangle,
like a letter saying
I keep all my promises.

A Ballad of the Northlands

seven snowflakes spun in air
—joined—
took on bone,
breath, feathers

The snow gull swept
the wide wastes
crying for the sea,
the sea

In a gale's confusion
she crashed to earth—
took on legs, arms,
skin and hair

The snow maid wandered
wandered
a waif of the drifts
till the castle folk found her

Such blue eyes,
such cold hands,
the prince murmured
and tried to warm her

lost himself a while
in her white arms,
in the fog of her voice
that knew only songs
of the wastelands

But always she yearned
for some far thing,
sea's salt
cloud's kiss

One day of snow
like a storm of feathers
the north wind came for her
chanted her unmaking

    skin to feathers
    song to cry
    bone to ice

seven snowflakes spun in air

The Last Mouse

I build my nests of useless silks,
shred the velvets into semblances
of my sisters' warm bodies
to lie against as I dream deep.
Only in sleep can I shed
these stiff, slow limbs,
putting on instead
sleek muscle, silver hooves.

When the queen's kind hands
reach down into my cage
each morning's store of pumpkin seeds,
I snort and rear, tossing my head,
reminding her of who I am
and where I've been,
the road we've shared.

The Daughter of Lir

When I was a girl
I watched the wild swans fly over
land and lake
and thought that wings
meant freedom.

An instant and our innocence
was cursed.

Laments we sang amid friends,
believing we knew sorrow
in our sorrow's childhood.
Unpeopled Sruth na Moile
tutored us so well
we took to our white breasts
centuries of silence.

Nine hundred years
without ceilis or keenings,
exiled to sky and sea,
no hearth or home
but our own feathered strangeness.

Brothers, brothers,
are you there?
Bleak Inis Gluaire
renders you invisible,
for who can discern
swans in snow?

Without you, there's nothing left me
but my own story.
I inscribe our histories
in the ice
with my black tongue.
My words part

the brittle grasses,
take shape upon
the frost of the lake
and rise into the air
like the lost Sidhe,

telling of jealousy and genesis,
of greed and grief,
the white beauty of death.

One-Winged

So what if I'm unfinished,
like the draft a poet thrusts inside his desk
when the rhymes won't come?
You think I weep in secret
for my missing arm?
I wear my one wing proudly,
never seek concealment in a baggy sleeve.

I will not call it curse.
Air was my element.
I breathed blue.

Our sister's suffering
enslaved us,
kept us circling above the castle
as if a silver chain pulled taut.

It took a leap of love
—no, call it fall—
to settle earthwards.

Claimed and tamed,
shut up whole in human skin,
my brothers forget those wilder realms,
lives bound to rule and reign,
clod and clay.

Every dawn I ascend the tower,
remove my shirt to feel the flutter
of feathers against heartbeat
before I unfold that last wing wide,
let the currents lift it, almost
freeing me from gravity.
It takes all I have
to resist wind's seduction.

Blame my sister?
How can you blame love that deep?
But I have learned
what costs I want to pay for love,
or to exact.

The woman who'll love me
will never need to hush
or burn,
her fingers will not bleed for me.
She will not tether me with sacrifice.

She too will cherish this wing,
knowing it has brushed the clouds,
certain I will always fly home,
hoping I will sing to her of sky.

The Island of Crows

On the Island of Crows
where winter summers,
the grass wears beads of ice in its hair
and snow humps the frosted shoreline

Blindfolded crows,
heads swathed in soiled shrouds,
stalk the beach in black masses
Some will tell you they augur good tidings,
their feathers black blessings
        They lie

Don't pity them their filthy plumage
torn to tatters
        They wait for you
Beneath those grey turbans
black eyes have already marked you

Some say the crows will tell your fortune
        Don't believe it
Don't approach with your penny
bright in your hand,
trusting as a child feeding bread to the ducks
        Keep clear of those beaks

When the mobs of visitors begin to dance,
        don't partake
Don't smile across the line at some stranger,
parrot him, crooked elbow for crooked elbow,
simulate his bent-kneed shuffle
        It is only a trick of the crows

You believe you're a tourist
who strolled with the crowds
across the bridge where summer waits,
in just steps you can return

to the shining side
      You are wrong

If the summer bridge re-appears,
      take it
run across to sun and smiles
to the city of clean whole lives
      Escape and forget

Meanwhile, keep your head up
and your eyes ahead
Never stop moving
Believe nothing you see or hear
      on the Island of Lies
though I am a hooded crow who tells you this

III. Awakened

Entreaty

Come sing to me a song, Neddir,
of time and the unburning worlds
for my mind dims
and I would remember.

Come, Neddir, let the notes of your flute
enter my mouth, renew my breath,
let your heart's drum startle
my heart awake.

Would you learn the secrets of the dark beyond?
I will share with you the stones' slow speech,
loosen my tongue with
worm-moistened syllables.

But first, sing to me of April's greening
for I feel the clutch of roots
but cannot sense the buds unfurling.
I have become December's daughter.

Come, Neddir, bend close to my grave,
let your sighs warm my flesh
that has grown so cold,
reach down and bring me forth.

For I grow weak but love is strong,
and there's no comfort
in forgetting.

Ariel's Release

No more for me
servitude's blue
balmy isles.

Wastes white as novitiates
tempt me.
My rude hollers
violate their pious silence,
crack the ill-tempered glaciers,
set the walrus' tusks a-quiver.

Or I navigate green channels
fathoms deep,
poke the empty sockets
of dead granddads
with impertinent fins
and mate the maelstrom.

No more the meek
and mincing chorister,
my laughter's thunder
topples bell-towers,
my cantillations frenzy
the cataracts.

I slither out
of flesh
to rise diffuse,
let myself fall
in liquid singularity,
one solitary raindrop.
O trembling transparency,
a self to harbor
rainbows in!

Subtlety may someday

bore me and I'll choose
to vault not merely space but time.
Re-attiring myself in corporeality,
as Parisian boulevardier I'll savor
croissant's buttery melt,
steam rising off my café crème
silvery as any sylph,
while a phonograph
husks, lusher than lagoons,
the blue voice of Billie Holiday.

Seeds of Love

Like any good farmer
I sowed in spring,
planting in dark earth
my beloved bone.
Now summer soil yields
new life upthrusting.
You rise, love, amidst the August corn,
awaiting September's ripening.
Those sealed lips will unclose.
And then, love, what harvest.

Noticed

Hey, boy—
you.
It was you who tugged me out,
your hair like the bravest
winter sunsets, the ones
simmering with summer.
I always hated to be cold.

Curious you, tracing my name,
saying it aloud,
wondering who I was.
"Poor thing," you said,
doing the math;
"she was only seventeen."

What could I do but come

offer you this August wind
in December,
this breath not-me and me,
not breath at all but never merely breeze?

With you, I might not have needed
the red braceleting my wrist,
the water going sunset-scarlet,
a lipstick shade I never
had the guts to wear.
I hated standing out.
I hated being invisible.

Say you would have noticed.
Say it would have been different.

You noticed.
What could I do but offer you
this something like

a kiss blown from a movie-star
stirring at your sunset hair?

Labyrinth of Sand

Under the wash of waves
my feet sink into the sand
but I do not drown

I walk the Sisters' labyrinth
that leads to the Heart of the Lake

Remember, you told me,
each night tracing the Sisters' Road
onto my back with gentle fingers
so I'd hold the pattern safe
within my body

In the firelight
I turned my face from you
but my skin welcomed your touch

Now my blood remembers,
my feet find the way

The wind across the lake
speaks with a voice like yours,
soft and sundered

For your brother's sake,
you said at first

And later,
For your sake,
I do this thing

High purposes and promises
The shoals on which hearts shatter

Soon all that mattered was the night,

whispers in firelight,
your fingers' journey across my back

I vow,
I'd told my brother,
I will win the Heart of the Lake,
source of the Sisters' power
and soon yours
No soul will live
to tell our secret

A drop, a drop,
with every step I swear I hear
droplets weep from my dagger
yet the lake's breast wears no red

Are all maps so costly,
all power so hard bought?

Soon, soon
I'll reach the Sisters' Tower,
my guilty hand will grasp the stone
three realms name
the Heart of the Lake

I will re-trace this watery path,
remembering the pattern
you taught me
And then?
My feet will find the world again
but my own heart henceforth
labors lost in labyrinth

Only one thing gladdens me:

Every night since I parted
you from breath,

the shadows thrown by firelight
bear a blessed familiarity,
my bare back has felt the trace
of your cold fingers

Lizzie Siddal's Blessing

Alive, I served his dreams.
A draught of the poppy
granted me release;
sleep came as easily as weeping.
And then no more, I thought,
would I have to play the muse.

No blessed damozel,
I never once
leaned down from heaven
or peered up from hell,
a load of lilies in my arms,
stars marring my brow,
demanding adoration.
If he pursued my image
down death's dark alleys,
it was no concern of mine.

Seven years after my burial
when hands reached down
into my grave,
I felt no surprise—

but oh, those hands reached past me,
past the hair he loved,
my gold-red hair still
growing bright about my bones,
to raise up
to light and life
only his abandoned manuscript.

I gave him a gift then,
set free into the skull-grey pages
a single golden strand of guilt.

Is that me crossing Cheyne Walk?

Do I fly into his hands on chaffinch wings,
giggle behind the garden door,
shimmer in the gaslight,
hover nightly at his bedside?
Neither oculists nor occultists
can cure him.
Long may he enjoy
my inspiration.

To a Gentleman Who is Visited

This ghost was anorexic
before the term was vogue,
so that is why your find your fridge
sighing its sour belly like a cave of winds,
your sesame noodles finished
before you're even home.
She eats so heartily now.

This ghost was told to disown and deny
her body, that was thin as rain,
and that is why she hopes
you will ignore her soft steps
heading to your bed, but not
the cool touch of unseen thigh
against your thigh
when you are shaking off your dreams.

This ghost was told
she had no voice for singing,
her hands were a cursed clumsiness,
and that is why you find
the pages of your Chopin ripped to snow,
the strings of your piano curdling out of tune
and yet, some mornings, Mozart sings
from keys now strangely whole.

This ghost was a daughter of poverty,
and that is why you discover
only your best silk shirts and ties
coiled like cut tongues on the closet floor,
and your silver cuff links are arranged
like prayer stones from an ancient rite.

This ghost was not taught to read
and that is why the pages of your *New Yorker*
turn by themselves on your nightstand,
and books disappear and then find themselves
returned to odd places,
dog-eared at the delectable passages.

But why me? you ask, why me?
Such blue eyes, she might answer,
or perhaps it is only your high ceilings,
wide closets, Hudson view,
that keep her here, somewhere
she would have chosen to live
if she'd been given choices.

Lapis Lazuli

lapis, I said,
and felt the stone dissolve warm
on my tongue.
you, too, tasted.

here is where
birds understand
the purpose of their wings
and the rose learns the art
of unfolding itself,
you said, and we gave
our blue tongues to each other.

here is where the center
of earth is, we said,
we are its axle,
double strands wed
to become single strand.
we are as holy as gravity.

we bit the stone again.
my hair grew so long in love
it swept the dust from the floor.
we bathed in the marble sarcophagi
and laughed the death from our flesh.
the secret of lazuli,
the secret of Lazarus.

here is where the stone remembers
and grows warm again.

Awakened

I slip out of never
into become,

garb myself in the mist
that rises from the old grass thirsting,
draw to me the hushing husks
of over-ready corn.

Dandelions' airy seeds
dance to me and cling,
the prickly leaves
grasp me like needy infants
seeking suckling.
Rocks' hardness I absorb,
the cold of stone,
claw and wing
of the storm-dashed starling
that flies no more.

From the drowsing village
I inhale the smoke of Samhain fires,
swallow their heat to make
a red heart beat,
build a new skeleton from
ashes born of the bones
of slaughtered cows.

Dreams drift
from the sleepers like sparks.
I consume,
sucking the subtle shapes,
all the forms of fear and guilt.
My muscles ripple
as I try on each one

and prowl amongst

the people I once knew,
unremembered,
soon to be acknowledged.
The eager hound of my shadow
bounds ahead.

I have borne the long dark,
and now I return,
trailing the darkness home.

IV. Invasion

The Art

There is an art to
supping in the dark.

The tango-stalk.
He leads, you follow,
Rogers to his Astaire,
your footsteps predicting
his stride's rhyme.
You match each hesitation,
the backward glance
determining that no one's there.

The blend.
Your breathing (you still call it that)
silent,
no tremor,
no waft of wispiest curl
betrays your blacker shadow shrouded
by the slouch of tenement and townhouse.
A jogger tugs the leash
of her curious Doberman
as they fleet past.
The doorman's lonely circle of light
doesn't find you.

The swoop.
If you had a pulse, how it would hammer.
Even so, within your veins
the blood (a storm of many rains)
surges like ocean waves
frenzied for more.
Now?
    Now!
Jaguars dawdle, owls laze.
Even you believe you must have wings.

The petrification.
Oh, that moment,
when his eyes widen in shock.
You're the pretty thing he'd hold a door for,
offer an umbrella to, protect from muggers.
With just your gaze
you administer paralysis,
don't even need to lie,
"You'll only feel a pinch."
You savor the racing heartbeat
under subdued flesh,
the jugular announcing its terror
and its invitation.

The slash.
Some playful tonguing
before you sink your fangs.
Adrenaline-high of the predator
rushes in before you even
have that first sweet taste.
Two thirsts are slaked.

All the rest is convenience.
Mere intake of nutrition.
Removal of the remains
(sexy as washing dishes).
I hate that part.

But ah, the art.

The Mummy Bared

Queenly robes,
the arms of lovers,
even skin's soft, elastic grip
she no longer can recall.

Lurching from alley to avenue
she clumps her clumsy way,
murmurs muffled beneath
numberless folds of linen
brittle as uninked papyrus.
She has forgotten words.

Empty,
she is empty,
nothing within
except the heart
missing its metronome.
She does not tick in time
with the rest of the earth's hours.
Like dream-people, she does not breathe;
the absent sound of inhale and exhale
dizzies her,
makes the world awry.
How could you miss so much
something you'd never really noticed?

This long wandering takes its toll:
she sloughs off wrappings
like a snake its skin,
yet no new supple self
emerges audacious and unblemished
in the wake of loss.
Her denuded brown feet
shrivel, mortified,
flesh laid bare in the most intimate revelation.

Another inch of cloth shreds;
with its end's unwinding
an amulet for luck in the afterworld
clinks to the pavement.
She hears it
but its music has no meaning;
she doesn't bend to retrieve it.
It would contain no clue
to what she's searching for:
her name,
even the most trivial memory—
whether faience beads or carnelians caressed her neck,
a dear friend's laugh,
the taste of figs,
was there a child?—
something of life,
something of self to hold onto.
Nothing comes.
Her wrappings trail her in the dirt
like the ribbons of a careless dancer.

Fumes of myrrh and cassia rise,
another amulet clinks to the ground,
as she unravels.

Kosode-No-Te

Cherry-sprigs on almond silk

    In the vintage clothing shop
    this kimono speaks to me

How kissing-ripe your lips will look
    against my cherries,
    it seems to say

"One hundred years old,"
the shop woman informs me.
"Very special."

The mirror shows me
    shuddering in its soft wings
    less courtesan than magic crane,
    face almond-pale,
    pupils widened to black moons
    as if already he stroked my silky skin

"Yes," I breathe.
  "Wrap it up."

It shimmers in its gauze nest,
fabric phoenix-egg,
before she shuts the box.

I bathe,
luxuriate in scented oils and steam,
powder my skin dry

bind up my hair in
unaccustomed pins
rouge my cheeks
bite my lips

to bid the cherries come
Clad in my kimono
I wait,
a silken prize,
precious orchid preserved
in a book of antique poems

"Honey, I'm—"

We've rendered him speechless,
my kimono and I

I open my arms
and he falls in

Silken whispers
Yessss, yessss

Long sleeves grasp him,
wrap him tight, tighter,
gather him to the kimono's bodice,
smother him in silk

he shudders

collapses,
body vacant as a suit on its hanger

Yessss, the silk whispers

The Cat Accursed

Avert your gaze
from my hobbled legs
shriveled paunch
spine carved into permanent arch
red skin flaking
flea-bitten, pustule-ridden
my lank fur falling out in clumps

Do you remember what I
once was
how fat and sleek and soft
how gold my eyes glowed
that day you placed me
in your baby's crib
to divert the demons' notice,
soak up each misfortune and affliction?

Spit three times and shudder
as I limp wheezing past
My sightless eyes don't need
to find you, I can sniff your guilt
don't need to hear you shrink
against the alley wall
your footsteps retreat from my shadow
as you run towards the light
your home
your good supper
that perfect, healthy child

Old Bone

Old Bone come soon

He come while sun too weak to argue
while wind's a scrabble of fingers
'long a banjo skin

Come ashiver in the wheeze of frogs
splutter up from silt and slough
through moss and murk
push past knobby cypress knees
like the river birthin' him

Old Bone slick
Come sliding up slow waters
easy as a gator slicin' duckweed
Even so, he set the hounds to ranting
raise their fur along their backs

He know them old songs
He know them tunes
full o' egrets' white ghost wings
and weepin'

Old Bone, thing he know best
is gaps
—loose fence-slats
chinks in window-frames
that big hollow opened up inside you
since that last gal done drop you

He know how sometimes
you eye them river deeps
thinking maybe down there's better

Old Bone like company
like to tote you down there

join his party in the crawfish mud
chuggin' river brew from gator skulls

Yeah, he know you

Old Bone come soon

Rusalka

Her tears pollute my river,
this ragged red-eyed girl
of swollen belly.
She wades into my waters.
Shock of human warmth stirs my chill,
blood-waves of the living soul.

I'd warn her away, make her leave,
but what else does she have?
She clutches the cradle of her
blossoming womb
and cries out,
a sob that spirals into feral wail,
before letting herself sink.

I cried that way once, I think,
in the days before my emergence
silenced even the dull frogs' chorus.

Her hair, so lovely now, slides
from its pins and undulates
like tentacles or seaweed.
I push the dead thing downstream.

Mine now the birches
and their pale limbs' reflections.
Mine the willows weeping,
heads bent against my banks.
Mine alone the drowned moon
whiter than the girl's flesh.

Max in Wolf-Suit

He sailed back, in and out of days.
Mommy hugged him,
Daddy fondled the tufted
wolfs' ears of his hooded PJs.

But, supper hot in his belly,
he could not forget starvation's pangs
before he'd learned to kill,
nights when he had scraped a pile
of leaves to make a bed,
shared with bats the refuge of a cave,
on that isle where time
stretched strangely.

New-old little body now tucked warm
beneath fresh-laundered sheets,
he imagined he could hear the birds scream
as he'd seized them from their nests,
the gush of blood down chin and chest,
taste of raw poultry foul in his mouth.

He hadn't won a kingship
just by staring into all their yellow eyes.
He scanned the little hands,
his arms and thighs,
re-blooming guileless pink,
for traces of the battle scars.

Staying king required
daily proof.
First to swing the vines,
best at hunt and howl,
strut and grunt,
there wasn't a chasm he hadn't leapt,
a boar he hadn't taunted.
He'd swum out farthest from the shore,

closest to the whirlpools,
bumping shoulders with the sharks.

When he came of age,
he had caressed chill
scale and beak,
descended into foetid fur,
risked claw wounds, love bites
piercing clear to bone.

One day his old boat bobbed
close to the coast.
He'd splashed to meet it,
grasped the tiller,
sailed in and out of years,
slipped the self
he'd come to think of as his own,
returned to this foreign country
called "home."

Max in his child-suit
waited for the skin to grow,
stretch as time had stretched.
The wolf-suit grew too,
inward and invisible,
fibers fusing with his soul.

The second time he came of age,
he was ready for it.

To love him was to mate
the hot and nervous nucleus of the cell.
But it was not all gleeful rumpus.

Too late I caught the lupine glare
behind the man-mask,
too late learned

he was still the wildest thing of all.

Invasion

Moon phases into full, pulling
me surer than the tides.

Her cratered face through porthole's
view mocks mine, altered, alien.

Our mission will abort, science
widowed of her astronauts,

for the silver bullet of our ship
cargoes its own infection—

me in wolfhide,
moondrunk, craving manflesh.

V.Attic Dust

The Emperor's Clockwork Song-Bird

Aroo, I'd sing for all unwanted things,
for the denizens of attics
and the citizens of rubbish heaps

—unhoned blades,
science texts from past decades,
last summer's sandals,
this week's scandals,
paper-dry spinsters,
unrepentant sinners,
loose-pegged mandolins with ruptured strings,
skeletons of birds with broken wings.

Upstart nightingale,
whose return caused my dethronement,
I could curse you!
—but you breathed your last long ago,
mere collage of bone and gristle,
cartilage and bloodied muscle.

Winter barely brushed your tail-feathers!
You endured at most a few weeks' hunger;
desires prodded your heart,
unanswered and unslaked,
perhaps five paltry years.

While I, I've known the creep
of rust through copper gears,
the loss of two—two!—ruby eyes,
dusty enamel scratched and pocked,
my peacock brilliance dulled to beige,
all the torment of the centuries' tick and tock.

Time's schooled me well in meter.
How my new-forged song would change!

No more the chipper ditty,
my aria would soar,
aged like wine in barrels
of sorrow and neglect—
for is this not the stuff
from which art's born?

I'd lay aside my arrogance
to shake your claw, old foe,
one musician to another,
and how I'd serenade you
—but no one seeks, much less finds,
that long-lost key that winds me.

Making Home

She has built this fortress
out of cat's cradles,
sepia photographs and chapel smoke

The bronze-green vase
given to her by the man from Prague
still whispers of mildewed stone and golems

The Balinese puppet strikes
a dead friend's poses,
dances to fragments of her favorite music,
creaks in sympathy with Brahms' *Requiem*

A dream-catcher straddles a window,
unwilling to let the oldest stories go,
its muttering constant as a stream in spring

A carved chair wears the imprint
of a love before betrayal,
its damask cushions still sagging
under familiar weight

Each precious unmatched china cup
radiates impressions of beloved lips

The largest wall is a mosaic,
tesserae of every treasured, broken thing
she's ever missed
That it fails to form a picture
doesn't bother her;
though she cannot come to terms with *wabi-sabi*,
unable to forget what's gone,
she embraces *kintsukurai*,
admiring what's flawed,
recognizing that sometimes empty space
—even more than gold—

can beautify and elevate,

aware of even objects'
sober journeys through the world

Attuned

Cradled between my legs,
your neck eased towards mine,
you sing and sob,
bass sighs sounding against my breastbone.

We three are one,
the music, the viol, and I,
holy trinity.

My fingers press and release
the strings,
draw the bow to ecstatic length
till our listeners bow their heads
to the linen-draped tables,
still as shrouds.

What do they hear?
The susurrus of island palms,
lullabies of long-dead mothers,
wronged lovers' cries?
Or is it not mere sound but all of sense
we give them,
so that they reel to meet red-cherry mouths
opening under pink-blossomed boughs,
lick the cream from pastry in a Budapest café?
Or do we move them beyond sense,
offer Music's promise of a better world,
priest's paradise, epicure's Elysium?

I gaze at them,
avoid the viol's carved head,
its cheeks of roseate wood,
unseeing eyes,
flowing locks and beard
modeled from your miniature.
The carving is a dead thing—

you're not there.

It's in the sound, the very soul
of the instrument, where you live again,
my lover, my teacher,
your blood poured in the varnish
in ancient orphic rite.
It's you who wake the viol
and give it voice.

It's you, locked between my thighs,
who turns mere notes to music,
you, my love, who taught me first
that every art requires sacrifice.

Braiding

The stolen ghost of you,
mute stand-in,
your shirt hangs white in the closet
wearing only its red-thread wounds,
thornless roses I once stitched
so you would guess I loved you

The scarlet flower that bloomed above your heart
looks like a bull's-eye, I realize
before I cut the knot that keeps it whole

Fingers deft as Penelope's,
I unpick a single thread,
unwhorl it, dedicate it like honed blade
to my devotions,

unbind my hair
Dark curls slip to my shoulders
like heavy serpents

Two long strands I pluck,
lay them alongside the red thread,
straighten them for the rite ahead,
witchery of hope
—love's purpose requires at least
the fallacy of smoothness—

pull the scarlet filament
taut as bowstring,

and begin to braid,
binding you to me

This act is not without cost,
no love ever is
It's not just our joys that join

I take unto me your wounds,
know soon I will kneel
with silver cup to catch the blood
where others' arrows lodge
as you will staunch my torn flesh,
staining your white cloths red

Once I wielded a silver knife,
        Soul-Skinner,
sharp as neglect,
its hilt incised with words
of love and praise withheld
For each lover, I slashed off
some scrap of my soul
till she limped, misshapen
queen of rags

But I have tossed away
my knife, renounced
diminishment

Now I braid
life to life,
knotting your heart to mine,
singing a song
of addition, completion

I am Ariadne reeling in her hero
towards the labyrinth's core
where he will soon embrace
her brother-self, that shaggy
rag-furred minotaur

The final knot is tied
Loose threads are one
This love cannot be undone

See in the shadows
the queen of rags enlarges,
dancing,
the red thread round her neck
incandescent as a string of rubies
or a rope of lies.

Straw Man

Wish-wakened, wind-hastened
wisp-whim—
here I am.
For what dark conspiracies
have you conjured me?

Don't use me long,
expect too much,
for I'm light-of-mind,
a harum-scarum fellow,
dusty husk not much
more substantial
than a moonbeam, ma'am.

Oh, so it's for that, then,
that you bid me rise
from my soft bed of self-stuff
and shake a leg?

I comply,
press your hands
between these vacant gloves,
tousle your hefty hair,
confide almost-somethings
into your ear.
Just don't request a
candlelit romancing;
where flames flaunt their fervor
you'll never find me.

Alas, now I'm the worse for wear.
One o'clock shadow shades
my rag-bag cheek,
a button eye
has popped its thread,
my wheaten locks scatter

to the four corners of the air.

Breeze bows me, madame,
at my waist.
I bid adieu
before your ardor
has undone me quite.

Psyche's Lamp

In this strange palace where seen things went unseen,
I had a mundane job to do:
to bring obscurity to light.
The tales say it was her astonishment,
setting her hand atremble,
that caused the drop of oil to fall.
But it was mine own.
Had I a mouth I would have gasped
when the circle of my illumination
revealed the monster
— dread eyes closed in sleep,
multi-hued wings folded
innocent as any napping dove's,
ivory hands clutching the quiver
of fateful weapons to his smooth flank —
blazing brighter than my own wick's burning.
I tipped toward that beauty,
drawn to it as I had drawn
dynasties of moths to my restive flame,
and scalded the unblemished shoulder.
Love awoke.
My fire extinguished in the hot breath
of his startled "Oh!"
Ever after, I would remain in darkness,
longing for another sight of Love,
waiting for the terrible god to rekindle me.

Penemue

When the Watchers sat in council,
determined to wreak havoc among humankind,
many were the instruments of destruction
we devised.

Azazel licked his lips,
and from one drop of shining spittle molded
curved scimitars sharp as hate,
neat stilettos,
ruby-pommeled sabers,
silver daggers etched with arabesques,
wicked switchblades quick as wit,
enough swords to ensure
an eternity of widows.

Gadriel wrung pigment
from his iridescent wings,
distilling creams and potions,
kohl and henna,
rouge to turn the wan girl ruddy,
powder to blanche the dusky, mole-pocked drab,
gloss to make lips blossom like post-coital roses.
He crowed over his jars,
foreseeing kingdoms ruined by men's lust,
women wasting themselves over each flaw
they imagined in their mirrors.

I, clever Penemue, plucked out one precious pinion,
scratched my arm deep, and from the opened vein
poured out lapis liquid,
thus fashioning the first ink-filled quill.
I gave God's children runes and alphabets,
clay for cuneiforms,
tablets and chisels,
inkstones and brushes,

paper and parchment,
pencils and pens,
ipads and styluses.
The Watchers rejoiced, envisioning riots incited,
treaties violated,
lawsuits ruining fortunes and families,
unseemly love letters breaking hearts.
I savored sweeter fare,
the dream-wearied author sunk in poverty,
the lion fearing each hit his last.
I would people palaces, attics, gutters
with blear-eyed poets
gnawing on the sour rind
of each
inadequate
word.

The Five Books

In the Library of Lyrinna
in the City on the Hill
there are five books.

First is the Book of Rooms.
Abandon the false index;
it never takes one to
the desired destination.
Instead, leaf through passages
on velvet chambers whose fur-heaped beds
promise easy slumber.
Or read of round chapels shaped
by candle-light and shadow;
between the lines of blurring type,
you'll swear you hear a chant
—your name, again, again,—
rise on hisses of glory like incense.

Second is the Book of Engines.
The illustrations set your pulse racing
as you dream of far travel,
impossible speeds.
Don't dare trace
the labyrinthal diagrams;
you'll set the gears ticking.
Should you cut yourself
on some sharp spoke,
your blood may wash across the woodcuts,
and then beware, beware,
what dread machinery you waken.

Within the furred cover of
the Book of Beasts,
you must pursue elusive words
that slip their herds to wander
amid scents of grasslands, brine,

monkey, hippogriff.
Keep your wits about you.
The careless finger may be crushed
by snapping jaws, a leaning elbow
slashed to ribbons by an errant claw.

Next is the Book of Sins.
Some Readers cry out that the pages burn,
others that they freeze like snow.

Last is the Book of Forgetting,
bound in nude ivory uncarved.
Each page is a puddle of black,
as if pulled newborn-wet from the press.
I stare into a pool of ink,
trying to forget the fate
of Yassinya the witch,
the Library's Creator and my beloved,
try to drown in black but still
I see her hair gleam gold
as the fire consumes her.

But no, let ink overwrite the scene,
douse the flames.
—Her burned face rises from the dark!—
I turn the page.

Black the ink
and black the page
and black the book
and black the world

In the Library of Lyrinna
in the City on the Hill
there are five books.

The Man Who Loved a Poem

The instant he read it, he loved it.
He adored its metaphors
marching across the page like an army
of black brides, exultant and shining.
He lauded its alliteration,
its loose and lovely vowels,
the queenly crooning of its consonants.
He admired its profundity.
It had changed his life.

He tore it from the book
and kept it in his pocket,
pulled it out six times each day,
wore its paper thin with caressing,
creased it to tatters with his constant
folding and unfolding, even though
he'd memorized it.

Once an hour, he declaimed it
loudly for friends and colleagues,
dramatically at cocktail parties
or on the occasional street-corner,
or softly to himself, such reverent whispers.

The poem, however, did not love him.
He didn't understand her.
He read her all wrong, stopping
at the ends of lines, ignoring
her enjambments.
His tongue poked
at her soft syllables.
She detested his incessant handling,
the probing of his dread eye.
Always, always, he put her
on display, acting like he owned her.

One night, when once again
he had laid her down upon his desk
in the lamp's cruel glare,
subject to his obsessive dissection,
she decided she'd had enough.

They found his body the next morning—
death by a thousand paper cuts.

And the poem? Gone,
flown out the open window,
free to pursue a million ears
or none,
but to a world without pockets.

Poppet Piracy

The cost of keeping you, my love,
is high.
    Blue candles worn to nubs,
    raven-throated nights of chanting,
    vats of honey to swim your name in
are the least of it.

To your symbol and substitute,
    carved poppet, blonde wool
    wound round waxen neck,
    I address my prayers and pleas.
Each time you falter,
your tiny twin, lumpen manikin,
    assures your return, as long
as the levy's paid.

If only I hadn't hidden him
    amongst my jewels.
He's contracted a lust for gems.
To keep your love fresh, he demands
    a price of pearls,
    an exaction of emeralds,
    a toll of tourmalines.

For each kiss I sacrifice a ruby,
    each embrace requires
    a bracelet's mocking clasp,
    and vows ring true only
    in gold bands' currency.

For tonight's caresses,
    adoring declarations,
what ransom will I pay?
My cupped hands tremble,
    sapphires at the ready.

Chopin's Heart

Stolen by Nazis,
hidden by priests,
surviving the onslaughts of war
as Warsaw fell around its tomb,
Chopin's heart, preserved in a jar
of cognac like fruit in a bottle of liqueur,
forebore the years, the visits
of the faithful.

Now scientists amass, eager
as crows on carrion.
Robed in the mysteries of formulae,
perfumed with formaldehyde,
they descend into the crypt,
pry open the vault
that's played nothing but rests
these two past centuries,
and assail the heart.

A few quick cuts,
the tiniest of samples,
and the organ's returned
to its jar, the wax resealed,
re-entombed.

What, they wonder,
does it have to tell them?
They ask and ask
but it doesn't speak.

Chopin's heart knows but
a single language,
not the one they're listening for.

It pronounces tender nocturnes
in the glare of the noontime lab,

singing of moonlit emeralds glinting
on Aurore's unclothed breasts.

The scientists continue probing,
attuned to their test-tubes,
to the samples simmering in chemical soups,
to the percussion of the computer's beeps.

The heart despairs,
wanders through minor-key impromptus,
a blizzard of sharps,
thunders in angry polonaises
that promise tigers rioting in Montmartre.

Deliberate Imperfection

The weaver chooses ivory
waves to chase each other
across cobalt borders for a sea.
On her grass-green ground
vermillion mountains loom,
almond arbors and lemon groves
settle their heavy limbs,
purple heliotrope shades
cities of citrine crickets,
brown hounds and their pups
overturn urns of sunflowers.

Now's the time
to weave a black strand
where a gold is due,
deliberate imperfection to
avoid the sin of hubris,
for only gods are perfect.
But she pauses,
thread in hand.
She loves her work too much
to mar it,
lets the gold strand keep its place.

Now's the time for *me* to weave.
From white clouds' complacent fleece
I pull the grayest threads,
twist them till I spin the blue sky black.
The southern breeze's first flirtations
form my warp,
my weft the keens of northern gusts.
My whips of lightning shuttle between strands
while the thunder-pedal booms.

My pattern emerges:
storm-struck trees,

roads collapsing to mud,
fields furrowed with rivulets
like the faces of widowers,
the village buried in rubble,
her broken loom.

Attic Dust

weightless as words
　　—and who knows the heft
　　　　of words better than I?—
I drowse, unformed,
　　　my crumbs unvisited

Long ago,
my creator kneaded Vltava clay
　　to a lump less lovely
　　　　than Sunday's challah

Scattering letters and crooning
　　the secret name of God,
　　　　Papa Loew spelled me alive.

Holy somnambulist,
　　I walked unthinking
　　　　acting only as he willed.

Till one day myself
　　awoke my self,
　　　　daring disobedience.

With a swipe of wool sleeve,
　　Papa Loew erased my word,
　　　　my breath,
　　　　　　reduced me again
　　　　　　　　to lump of clay.

　　Below the synagogue's rafters,
　　the backwards-racing clock,
　　　　I sleep
　　　　　　while Parízská Street laughs or screams
　　　　　　　　to the beat of axes or hammers
　　　　　　　　　　Tourists shuffle murmuring
　　　　　　　　　　　　past prayer-books and gravestones

But what is truth? What is death?
   Emet, met
What is life? What is sleep?

In dreams my tongue
     untwists
       and I hold forth
       erudite as a rabbi,
           charming as a matinee idol.

No longer lumbering,
    my grace outslinks
            the mayor's cat.

My mud, Brother Adam, like yours
         decays to dust.

And
this dust
     dreams.

Acknowledgements

The following poems originally appeared in these publications:

The Bone-Joiner – *Kaleidotrope*, Winter 2016

Ah, Joringel! – *Goblin Fruit*, Spring 2012

The Gifts – *Mithila Review*, issue 7, January 5, 2017

Dr. Chadpur Goes Fishing in the Animasphere – *Polu Texni*, August 1, 2016

On Failure's Wings – *Mirror Dance*, issue 32, Winter 2015

Birdspell – ©2018 by Sandi Leibowitz. First publication, original to this anthology.

Ephemera – *Lakeside Circus*, March 15, 2016

Sun-Taste – ©2018 by Sandi Leibowitz. First publication, original to this anthology.

Sycorax Awaits the Birth of Caliban – *Jabberwocky*, issue 13, September 2012

Witch-Love – *Liminality*, issue 12, Summer 2017

Sleeping Gypsy – *Star*Line*, issue 36.4, Autumn 2013

Lady Mary Speaks of Dreams – *Niteblade*, volume 25, September 2013

Im Wald – *Mythic Delirium* 3.2, October-December 2016

A Ballad of the Northlands – *Rose Red Review*, Summer 2013

The Last Mouse – *Magazine of Speculative Poetry*, vol. 9, no. 3, Fall 2013

The Daughter of Lir – *Mythic Delirium*, issue 26, Spring 2012

One-Winged – *Mythic Delirium*, issue 2.4, April-June 2016

The Island of Crows – *Niteblade*, volume 33, September 2015

Entreaty – *Liminality*, issue 2, December 2014

Ariel's Release – *Mythic Delirium* 2.1, July 2015

Noticed – ©2018 by Sandi Leibowitz. First publication, original to this anthology.

Seeds of Love –*Dreams and Nightmares*, issue 96, September 2013

Labyrinth of Sand – *Niteblade*, volume 28, June 2014

Lizzie Siddal's Blessing – *The Golden Key*, issue 2, Summer 2013

To a Gentleman Who is Visited – *Apex Magazine*, issue 31, December 6, 2011

Lapis Lazuli – *Abyss and Apex Magazine of Speculative Fiction*, issue 45, First Quarter 2013

Awakened – *Niteblade*, issue 29, September 2014

The Art – *Niteblade*, volume 30, November 2014

The Mummy Bared – *Polu Texni*, July 18, 2016

Kosode-No-Te – *Liquid Imagination*, November 28, 2013

The Cat Accursed – *Niteblade*, volume 18, December 2011

Old Bone – *Mythic Delirium* 0.3, January 2014

Rusalka – *Not One of Us*, issue 56, September 2016

Max in Wolf-Suit – *Kaleidotrope*, Spring 2016

Invasion – *Rose Red Review*, Autumn 2013

The Emperor's Clockwork Songbird – ©2018 by Sandi Leibowitz. First publication, original to this anthology.

Making Home – *Pantheon*, Hestia issue, November 2016

Attuned – ©2018 by Sandi Leibowitz. First publication, original to this anthology.

Braiding — *Niteblade*, volume 27, March 2014

Straw Man — *Strange Horizons*, January 28, 2013

Psyche's Lamp — *Eternal Haunted Summer*, Winter Solstice issue, December 2016

Penemue — *Mirror Dance*, Summer 2013

The Five Books — *Mirror Dance*, Spring 2016

The Man Who Loved a Poem — *Silver Blade*, Summer 2015

Poppet Piracy — *Melancholy Hyperbole*, October 6, 2013

Chopin's Heart — *Polu Texni*, March 2014

Deliberate Imperfection — ©2018 by Sandi Leibowitz. First publication, original to this anthology.

Attic Dust — *Silver Blade*, issue 21, February 2014

About the Author

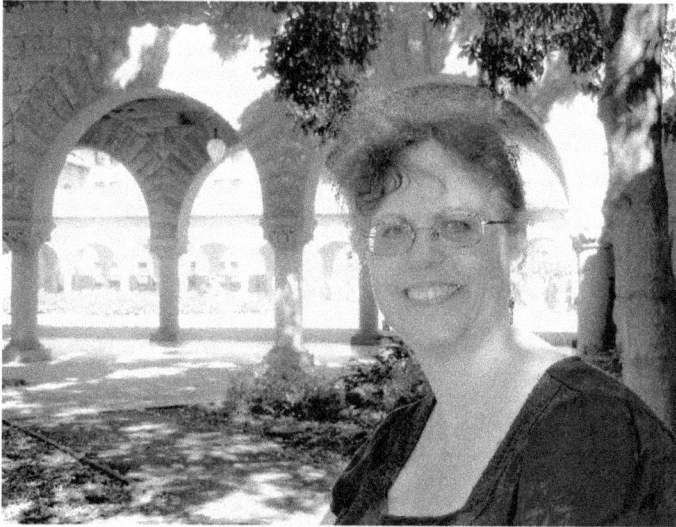

Sandi Leibowitz lives in a raven's wood, next door to bogles, in New York City. A voice major at Manhattan's High School of Music and Art, she received a B.A. in English from Vassar College, an M.A. in English from NYU, post-baccalaureate certification in teaching from William Paterson, and an M.L.I.S. from Rutgers. After a variety of jobs (including ghostwriting for a monsignor and working behind one of the caribou dioramas at the Museum of Natural History), she is now an elementary-school librarian, which enables her to hook kids on reading, tell stories, and play with puppets. She also sings classical and early music and plays recorders.

Her speculative fiction and poems may be found in *Liminality*, *Through the Gate*, *Metaphorosis*, *Mythic Delirium*, *Luna Station Quarterly*, *Apex*, *Kaleidotrope*, *Gaia: Shadow and Breath 3*, *Strange Horizons*, *Goblin Fruit*, Ellen Datlow's *Best Horror of the Year 5*, and other magazines and anthologies. Her poems have been nominated for the Pushcart Prize, Rhysling, and Best of the Net awards; two won second- and third-place Dwarf Star Awards.

Sandi invites you to visit her at **www.sandileibowitz.com**.